KING COBRAS

by Katie Marsico

Children's Press®

An Imprint of Scholastic Inc.
New York Toronto London Auckland Sydney
Mexico City New Delhi Hong Kong
Danbury, Connecticut

Content Consultant
Dr. Stephen S. Ditchkoff
Professor of Wildlife Sciences
Auburn University
Auburn, Alabama

Library of Congress Cataloging-in-Publication Data
Marsico, Katie, 1980–
  King cobras / by Katie Marsico.
      pages cm.—(Nature's children)
  Includes bibliographical references and index.
  Audience: Ages 9–12.
  Audience: Grades 4–6.
  ISBN 978-0-531-20978-3 (lib. bdg.)
  ISBN 978-0-531-24304-6 (pbk.)
  1. King cobra—Juvenile literature. I. Title.
  QL666.O64M366 2013
  597.96'42—dc23   2012034328

King Cobras

Class	Reptilia
Order	Squamata
Family	Elapidae
Genus	*Ophiophagus*
Species	*Ophiophagus hannah*
World distribution	China, India, Indonesia, Malaysia, the Philippines, and Vietnam
Habitat	Warm, humid environments, including tropical rain forests and swamps; some are also found in grassy plains and foothills
Distinctive physical characteristics	Extra skin around the neck flares into a hood to scare enemies; forked tongue; fangs; lower jaw can unhinge to make room for large prey; scales in shades of black, brown, gray, and green; yellowish or cream-colored underside; long, muscular body
Habits	Builds nest of twigs, leaves, and sticks that is used to safeguard clutch of eggs; can raise one-third of its body off the ground when preparing to strike; generally prefers to flee rather than fight; growls by forcing air through the space between its vocal cords; sheds skin every few months; swallows prey whole; uses its fangs to inject prey with venom
Diet	Prefers to feed on pythons and rat snakes, but will eat other cobras and kraits; also eats birds, lizards, small mammals, and eggs

KING COBRAS

Contents

CHAPTER 1

Long and Lethal

The noises of countless animals echo across a rain forest in western India. Monkeys screech and tropical birds call out over the treetops. A tiger lets loose a thunderous roar. But the forest suddenly slips into silence after a low moan is heard rumbling through the dense **undergrowth**.

It almost sounds like a dog is growling. But the source of the noise is far fiercer. Soon, a king cobra flares its hood and opens its mouth to reveal its deadly fangs. Any creatures close by have good reason to be afraid. They have been caught in the path of the largest **venomous** snake in the world.

King cobras are **reptiles** known for their size and their toxic bite. These snakes pump enough venom through their fangs to kill an Asian elephant.

A king cobra preparing to strike can be a terrifying sight.

Deadly Looks

King cobras usually reach a length of 12 to 15 feet (3.7 to 4.6 meters). Some have been known to grow longer than 18 feet (5.5 m). They typically weigh about 20 pounds (9.1 kilograms). Males tend to be larger than females.

There are few fiercer sights than a king cobra flaring its hood and revealing its fangs. Its neck is 1 foot (0.3 m) wide when flared. Its fangs each measure 0.5 inches (1.3 centimeters) long. The snake's skin is covered in scales from head to tail. These scales are various shades of black, brown, gray, and green. Most king cobras have a yellowish or cream-colored underside. Some also have white or yellow bands that stretch along the length of their bodies. The patterns and coloring of the snake's scales seem to depend on the snake's age and where it lives.

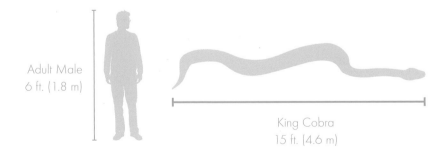

Adult Male
6 ft. (1.8 m)

King Cobra
15 ft. (4.6 m)

Some king cobras, such as the one pictured here, have dark undersides.

The Range of a Dangerous Reptile

Wild king cobras are mainly found in India, China, Vietnam, Indonesia, Malaysia, and the Philippines. They are able to survive in a variety of habitats within this range. However, they generally prefer the warmth and humidity of a tropical environment. King cobras are cold-blooded. This means that their body temperature is affected by the outside temperature. King cobras become too weak to hunt if they get too cold.

A large number of king cobras live in rain forests or swamps. Others roam Asia's plains and grassy foothills. It is not uncommon for them to spend time in areas that are located along a body of water.

King cobras frequently slither through the undergrowth. Thick patches of shrubs and bushes provide them with shade from the sun. These snakes also climb trees and can swim across rivers and streams.

King cobras are strong swimmers.

CHAPTER 2

Incredible Adaptations

King cobras have several **adaptations** that help them escape enemies and hunt down **prey**. King cobras mainly hunt pythons and rat snakes. They also eat other cobras and **kraits**. Sometimes they hunt birds, lizards, or small **mammals**.

Like most snakes, a king cobra does not rely on its nostrils to sniff out prey. It instead picks up scent particles by flicking its forked tongue in the air. It then brushes its tongue against the Jacobson's organ. This is a special sense organ on the roof of its mouth. It sends electrical signals to the snake's brain. These signals help the snake process information about nearby smells.

King cobras also locate prey using their sharp eyesight. They can spot motion from as far as 330 feet (101 m) away. King cobras do not have outer ears. But they are still extremely sensitive to the vibrations caused by sound waves.

A king cobra largely depends on its tongue to detect the presence of prey.

Attacking and Eating

A king cobra kills its prey with the help of deadly venom. Special **glands** located behind its eyes produce the toxins that flow through its short, hollow fangs. Some other snakes have more powerful venom. Yet this does not make king cobras any less deadly. They simply deliver a larger dose of venom when they strike.

Just one bite from a king cobra **paralyzes** prey. It takes only minutes for the venom to shut down body systems that control breathing and blood flow. The king cobra then swallows its victim whole. It can unhinge its jaw and stretch its throat and stomach to make room for larger prey.

King cobras can go several months without eating after a big meal. This is because their bodies take a long time to break down food into energy.

FUN FACT! A king cobra's venom also helps the snake digest, or break down, food in its stomach.

After paralyzing this mouse, a king cobra prepares to swallow it whole.

16

Remarkable Movement

King cobras are agile and amazingly flexible. Much of a king cobra's body is made up of powerful muscles. Several pairs of ribs are connected to the snake's spine. Snakes do not have feet or claws. Instead, they use their scales to grip surfaces. These physical features allow king cobras to climb trees, swim across water, and quickly strike out at prey.

A king cobra can raise one-third of its body straight off the ground when it is ready to attack. If hunting, it thrusts its fangs downward into its victim's flesh. In other situations, the snake relies on this lifting motion to threaten enemies.

Adult king cobras do not have to worry about many predators. Human beings and small animals called mongooses are the only threats they face. Generally, king cobras try to flee if they feel cornered. But they position themselves to attack if escape is impossible.

King cobras sometimes climb trees to avoid danger.

Keep Away

Most animals try to steer clear of the king cobra. Its size is usually enough to keep enemies at a distance. A king cobra that measures 18 feet (5.5 m) from head to tail is longer than an average minivan! Attacking and killing an animal this large presents a challenge for potential predators.

A king cobra can also warn enemies away by flaring the muscles and bones in its neck. This causes extra skin around its head to stretch. The result is the king cobra displaying a hood that tells predators to stay away.

The king cobra's low growl sends a similar message. It takes a deep breath in and then tightens its body. This forces air through the space between its vocal cords and creates the snake's unmistakable warning moan.

Mongooses are among the few animals that king cobras do not always succeed in frightening away.

Smart Snakes

Many scientists consider king cobras to be the smartest snakes in the world. They have observed several behaviors in king cobras that are unlike those of other snakes.

Animal experts who have spent time with king cobras believe that they show an amazing awareness of their surroundings. In **captivity**, they have demonstrated that they are able to tell their caregivers apart from complete strangers. Wild king cobras are famous for being conscious of one another's **territory**. King cobras also build nests to protect their eggs. No other snakes do this.

Most scientists are eager to continue studying king cobras. They want to learn more about how these ferocious predators use their brains to learn and adapt to their surroundings.

FUN FACT! King cobra nests have two separate chambers. A lower one holds the eggs and an upper one has space for the mother.

Scientists hope to learn more about king cobras' level of intelligence.

CHAPTER 3

A Look at a Life Cycle

King cobras are **solitary** animals. They do not need to live in a group for protection because they have few natural predators. Instead, king cobras can be extremely territorial. This means that one animal is often willing to fight another for control of a certain area. King cobras that are behaving in a territorial manner use their heads to wrestle one another. Whichever snake manages to push its opponent's head down first is the winner.

King cobras sometimes come together with other members of their **species** for reasons other than fighting. Their **mating** season usually takes place between January and March. Female king cobras release natural chemicals called pheromones at the beginning of the season. The males use their Jacobson's organs to detect the pheromones and track down nearby females that are ready to mate.

King cobras rarely spend time together peacefully unless it is time to mate.

Unique Nest Builders

One of the things that make king cobras so unique is the way they care for their eggs. The female lays between 20 and 50 eggs a few months after mating. They rest in a pile of twigs and grass that she has pulled together using her coils. Most other snakes do not take this much effort to guarantee the survival of their young. It is not unusual for other snake species to immediately abandon their eggs after laying them.

A female king cobra carefully guards her clutch for two to three months. Sometimes her mate joins her. King cobras need to be on the lookout for mongooses, monitor lizards, and other animals that feed on their eggs. Elephants are also a threat. They have been known to accidentally trample snake nests.

Adult king cobras usually leave just before the eggs hatch. Scientists believe they do this to avoid eating their own young.

By the time a young king cobra hatches, its parents have usually left the nest.

Fierce from the Start

King cobra babies are not nearly as large as their parents. This does not make them any less ferocious. Young king cobras are already aware of their surroundings shortly after they hatch. They do not hesitate to display their hoods as a warning if they feel threatened.

Baby king cobras measure around 14 inches (35.6 cm) long and 0.5 inches (1.3 cm) wide. They are often shiny black with thin bands of yellow scales. This coloring usually changes as the snakes grow older.

A young king cobra is able to survive on its own from the moment it hatches. It does not go hungry even though its parents are gone and it is not quite ready to begin hunting. This is because king cobra babies have a special pouch in their stomach called a yolk sac. The yolk sac provides them with nourishment.

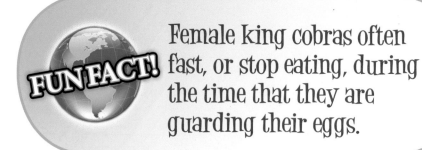

FUN FACT! Female king cobras often fast, or stop eating, during the time that they are guarding their eggs.

Baby king cobras may be small, but they are very independent.

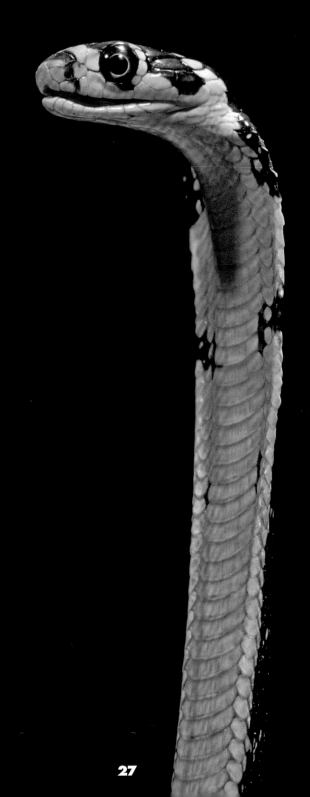

Approaching Adulthood

King cobras begin hunting roughly 10 days after birth. These young snakes already produce venom that is potent enough to paralyze and kill prey. Young cobras have to be careful because they are still small. Mongooses, army ants, and giant centipedes have all been known to kill young king cobras. King cobras face fewer wild predators as they start to get bigger.

The snakes begin to regularly shed their skin as they grow larger. Shedding allows reptiles to continue growing and keeps their scales healthy. Young king cobras go through this process every month. Adults do not shed as often.

A king cobra reaches adulthood when it is four to six years old. This is also about the same time that it is ready to mate. Wild king cobras live for around 20 years.

A king cobra's eyes often turn bluish-gray shortly before it sheds its skin.

CHAPTER 4

From Prehistory to the Present

Snakes first appeared about 150 million years ago. Dinosaurs still walked the earth during this time. Scientists believe that snakes are related to early lizard species. It is possible that the earliest snakes lived in water and had legs. They moved onto land and began to change form over time. Around 2,900 snake species live in the world today.

About 300 of these snake species are venomous. Experts suspect that venomous snakes have existed for roughly 60 million years. No one knows the exact date that king cobras first appeared. However, they were first described by European scientist Thomas Edward Cantor in 1836.

The king cobra's scientific name is *Ophiophagus hannah*. This name sums up the snake's diet and behavior in Greek. *Ophio* translates to "snake." *Phagus* means "eater." The term *hannah* is related to trees and forests. Altogether these words correctly identify king cobras as animals that eat snakes and often live in the forest.

This prehistoric snake fossil was found in Wyoming.

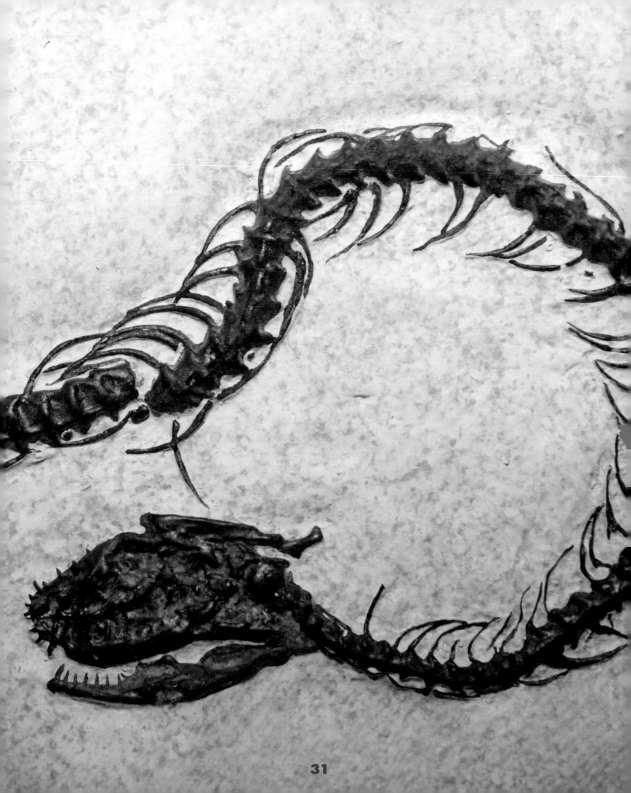

A King Cobra's Close Relatives

The king cobra belongs to the elapid family. This family includes coral snakes, sea snakes, mambas, kraits, tiger snakes, and cobras. All elapids are extremely venomous and have short fangs that cannot move.

There are around 20 species of what are called true cobras. They are close relatives of the king cobra. But king cobras are not in the same genus as these snakes.

Several physical differences set the king cobra apart from its close relatives. For instance, king cobras are usually larger than true cobras. True cobras also have shorter, wider hoods. In addition, the scales on a king cobra's neck form a unique design. Most cobras have a circular scale pattern that almost resembles an eye or a pair of eyes. A king cobra has an arrow-shaped stripe on its neck instead. Finally, the king cobra has a pair of large scales on the back of its head. True cobras do not have these scales.

Red spitting cobras are true cobras that live in Africa.

Differences Within a Single Species

There is currently only one official species of king cobra. But not all of these snakes are identical. Their size, coloring, and markings depend on where they live.

For example, king cobras in western regions tend to be various shades of brown and black. Their scales form patterns of dark bands that gradually fade as the snakes age. King cobras living in southern areas are usually brown, gray, and green. They often do not have any bands at all. They are generally larger than king cobras found in northern regions.

Experts believe that these physical differences are the result of adaptations to individual environments. Scientists have discussed the possibility of organizing king cobras into more than one species in the future. For now, their main concern is making sure that human activity doesn't cause these snakes to disappear forever.

King cobras from places such as China usually have darker skin than others.

CHAPTER 5

Trying to Live Together

King cobras share a complicated relationship with human beings. People in certain parts of India and Southeast Asia consider them sacred. King cobras are believed to control everything from rainstorms to farm crops.

Other people are not so respectful of king cobras. Humans pose several threats to these snakes. People hunt and kill them for many reasons. The biggest danger they face at the hands of humans is deforestation. This happens when people cut down trees and clear swamps and grasslands. They do this to construct roads, buildings, and farms.

King cobras are losing large portions of their natural habitat in the process. This makes it harder for them to successfully hunt and breed. Deforestation also drives king cobras out of the wild and closer to areas where people live and work.

Some farmers clear their land by burning down trees and underbrush.

Human Impact

Not everyone realizes that most king cobras would prefer to avoid contact with humans. People often kill them out of fear or misunderstanding. But king cobras are rarely responsible for human deaths. They would rather run away than fight people.

Hunting is another threat to these snakes. People in some parts of the world eat the king cobra's meat. They also use its skin to make clothing. Its **bile** and venom are ingredients in various medicines. The pet trade has also had a negative effect on king cobras. People remove these snakes from their natural environment. They then sell the cobras to buyers who are fascinated by the idea of owning an **exotic** pet.

Experts are not certain exactly how many king cobras currently exist in the wild. Scientists believe that the king cobra population has probably decreased by about 30 percent over the past 75 years.

Some people keep king cobras and other types of cobras and perform with them on the street to make money.

King Cobra Conservation

More people are beginning to support efforts to protect king cobras. Conservationists are trying to educate the public about these snakes and how human beings can have a serious impact on their survival. One famous example of this is the work of scientist Romulus Earl Whitaker. He founded the Agumbe Rainforest Research Station in western India in 2005. Whitaker created the station to study king cobras in their natural habitat. He and his fellow conservationists hope to use what they learn to help the snakes continue to survive in the wild.

King cobras are not in immediate danger of extinction. This could change in the future if humans do not do their part to protect both the species and the environment. It is important to remember that king cobras are more than just the world's largest venomous snakes. They are also unique and remarkable animals that deserve protection and respect.

Romulus Earl Whitaker has worked to protect reptiles for many decades.

Words to Know

adaptations (ad-ap-TAY-shuhnz) — changes that living things go through so they can fit in better with their environments

agile (AJ-il) — able to move fast and easily

bile (BILE) — a digestive juice produced by the liver

captivity (kap-TIV-i-tee) — the condition of being held or trapped by people

clutch (KLUHCH) — a nest of eggs

conservationists (kon-sur-VAY-shun-ists) — people who work to protect an environment and the living things in it

environment (en-VYE-ruhn-mint) — surroundings in which an animal lives or spends time

exotic (ig-ZAH-tik) — unusual and fascinating

extinction (ik-STINGKT-shun) — being completely wiped off the planet

family (FAM-uh-lee) — a group of living things that are related to each other

genus (JEE-nuhs) — a group of related plants or animals that is larger than a species but smaller than a family

glands (GLANDZ) — organs in the body that produce natural chemicals

habitats (HAB-uh-tats) — the places where an animal or a plant is usually found

humidity (hyoo-MID-i-tee) — the amount of moisture in the air

kraits (KRITZ) — brightly colored and extremely venomous Asian snakes mammals (MAM-uhlz) — warm-blooded animals that have hair or fur and usually give birth to live young

mating (MAYT-ing) — joining together to produce babies

paralyzes (PEHR-uh-ly-zez) — causes another animal to be unable to move

predators (PREH-duh-turz) — animals that live by hunting other animals for food

prey (PRAY) — an animal that's hunted by another animal for food

reptiles (REP-tilez) — cold-blooded animals that usually have a backbone and scales and lay eggs

sacred (SAY-krid) — very important and deserving great respect

solitary (SOL-ih-tehr-ee) — preferring to live alone

species (SPEE-sheez) — one of the groups into which animals and plants of the same genus are divided

territory (TER-i-tor-ee) — area of land claimed by an animal

undergrowth (UHN-dur-grohth) — plant life that grows beneath the tall, mature trees in a forest

venomous (VEN-nuh-muhss) — poisonous

Habitat Map

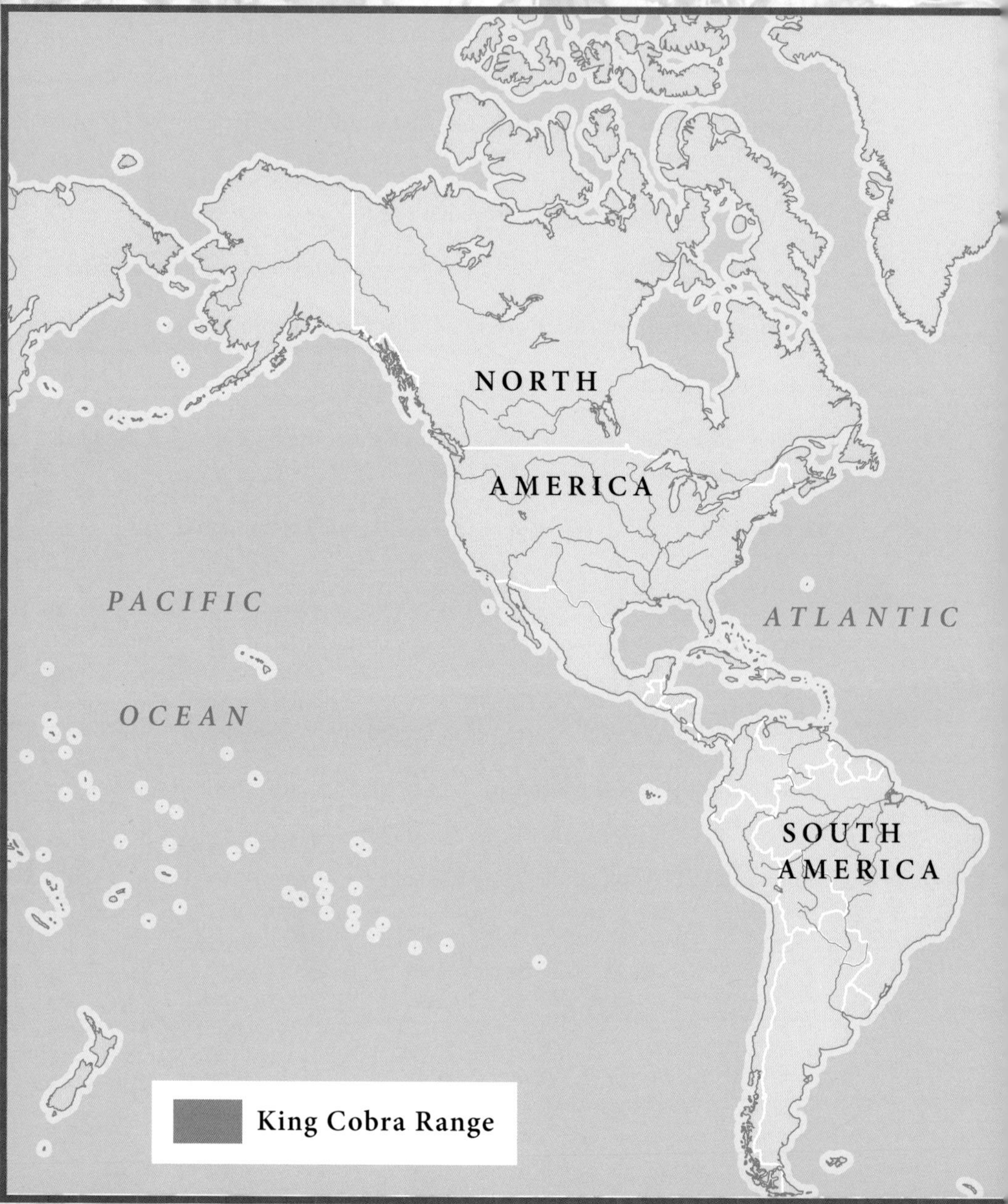

NORTH

AMERICA

PACIFIC

ATLANTIC

OCEAN

SOUTH
AMERICA

King Cobra Range

ARCTIC OCEAN

EUROPE

ASIA

AFRICA

PACIFIC OCEAN

INDIAN OCEAN

OCEAN

AUSTRALIA

Find Out More

Books

Jackson, Tom. *Deadly Snakes*. New York: Gareth Stevens Publishing, 2011.

Graham, Audry. *King Cobra*. New York: Gareth Stevens Publishing, 2011.

Owings, Lisa. *The King Cobra*. Minneapolis: Bellwether Media, 2012.

Visit this Scholastic Web site for more information on king cobras:
www.factsfornow.scholastic.com
Enter the keywords **King Cobras**

Index

Page numbers in *italics* indicate a photograph or map.

About the Author

Katie Marsico is the author of more than 100 children's books. She is fascinated by king cobras but hopes to never get too close to one. Ms. Marsico dedicates this book to two of the biggest snake fans she knows—Jack and Anthony Sebastian.